Down The Road

by

Bob Carlson

Copyright © 2016
ISBN: 978-0-9972220-5-0
Published by Carlson Press

carlsonsketch@gmail.com

ART **KRYPTO**

ART **KRYPTO**

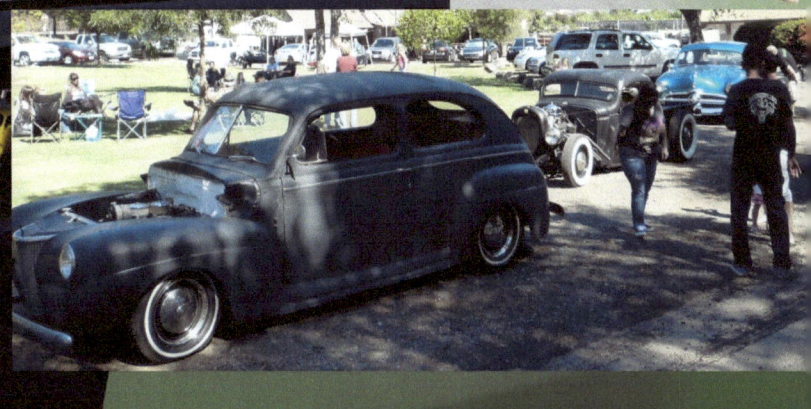

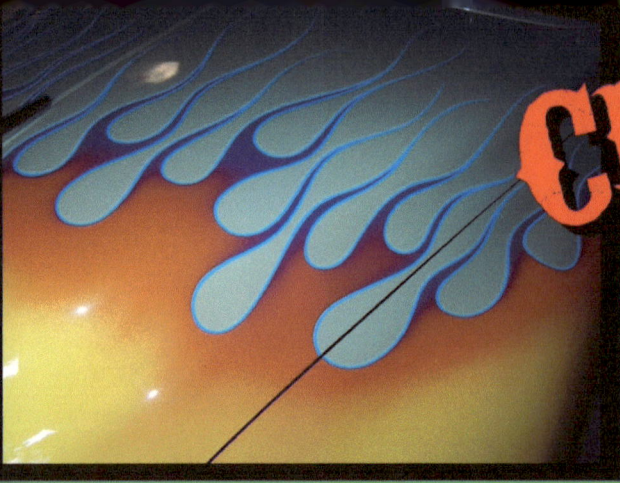

CHET

CHET

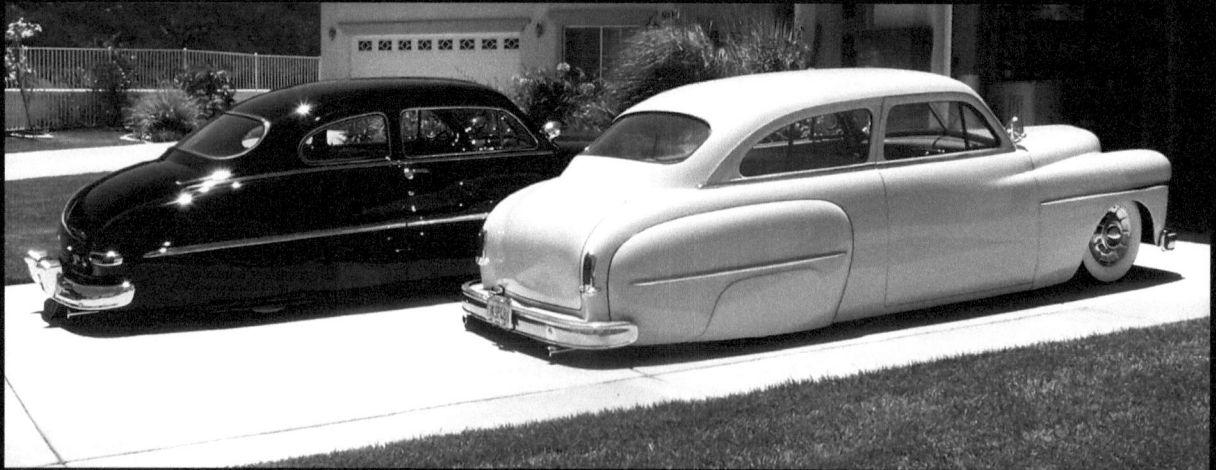

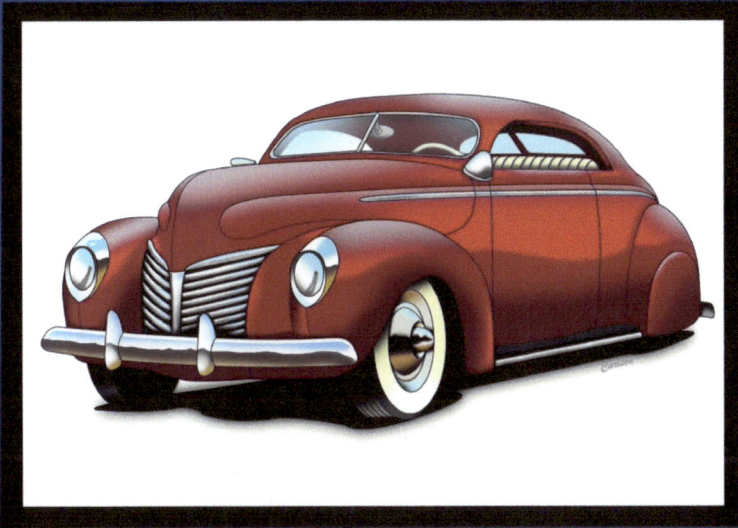

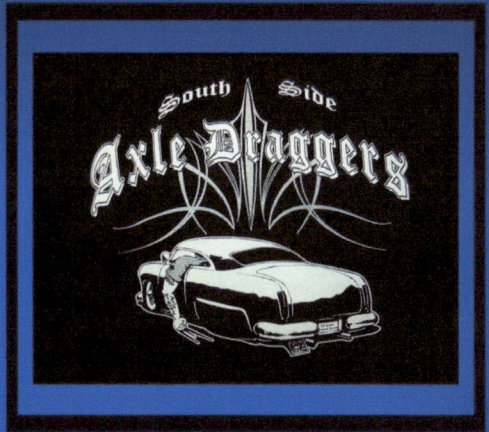

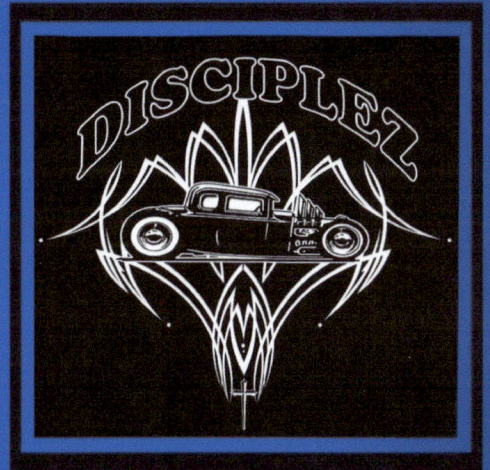

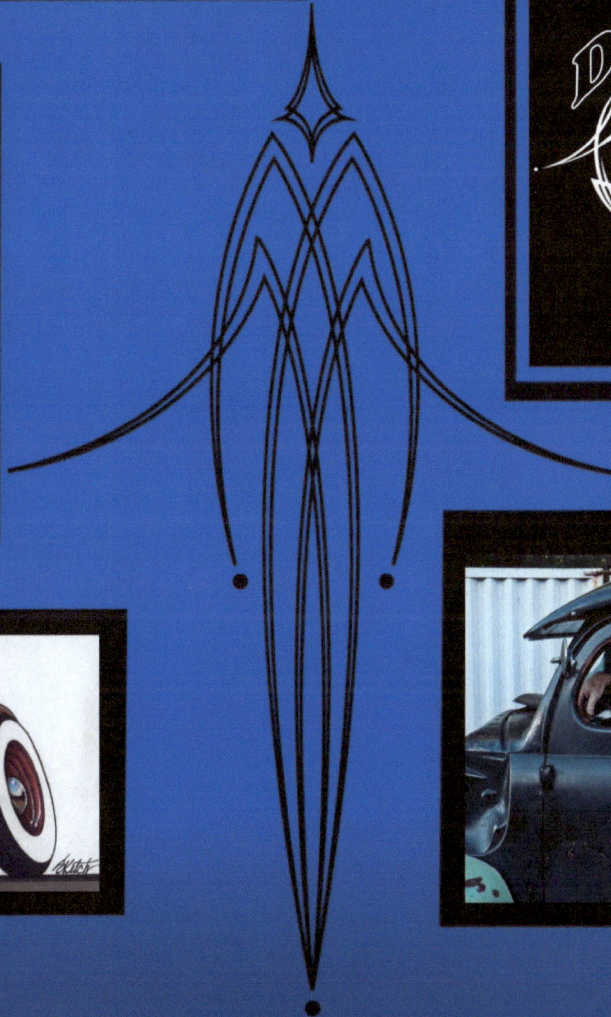

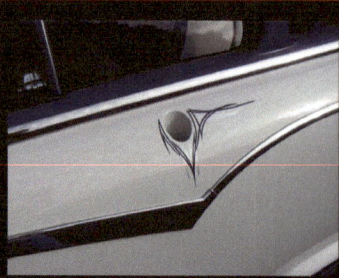

Perris Dan

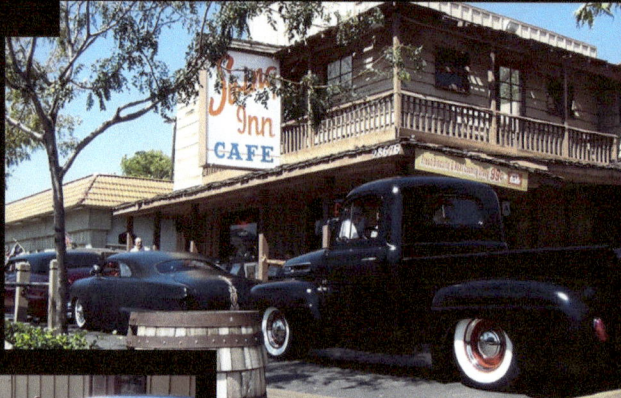

Sunnyside

Price

UTAH

Humboldt-Toiyabe
National Forest

Richfield

Cedar City

Staircase-Escalante   Recreation

St George   Springdal

Mesquite

Winslow   Holbrook

Death Valley
National Park

Las Vegas

Henderson

Lake Mead
National
Recreation
Area

Grand Canyon
National Park

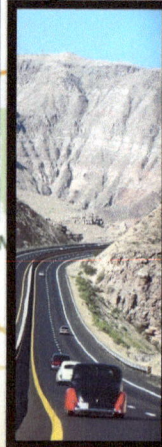

695 miles

Los Angeles

Anaheim   Riverside

Long Beach   Palm Desert

Temecula, CA

Sedona

Cottonwood

ARIZONA   Show Low

Pinetop-Lakeside

Tonto National
Forest

Phoenix

Tattoo Greg

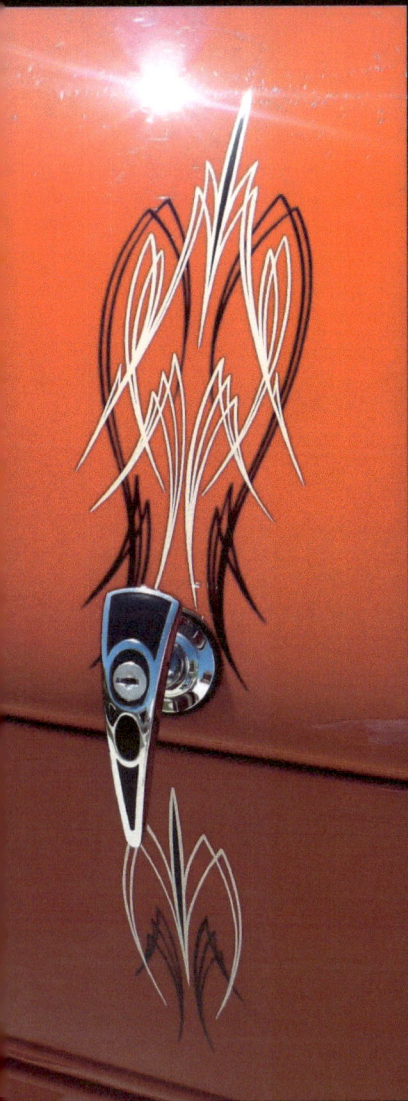

GAS & DIESEL
RAINBOW OAKS SQUARE 1 MILE

Disciplez c.c.

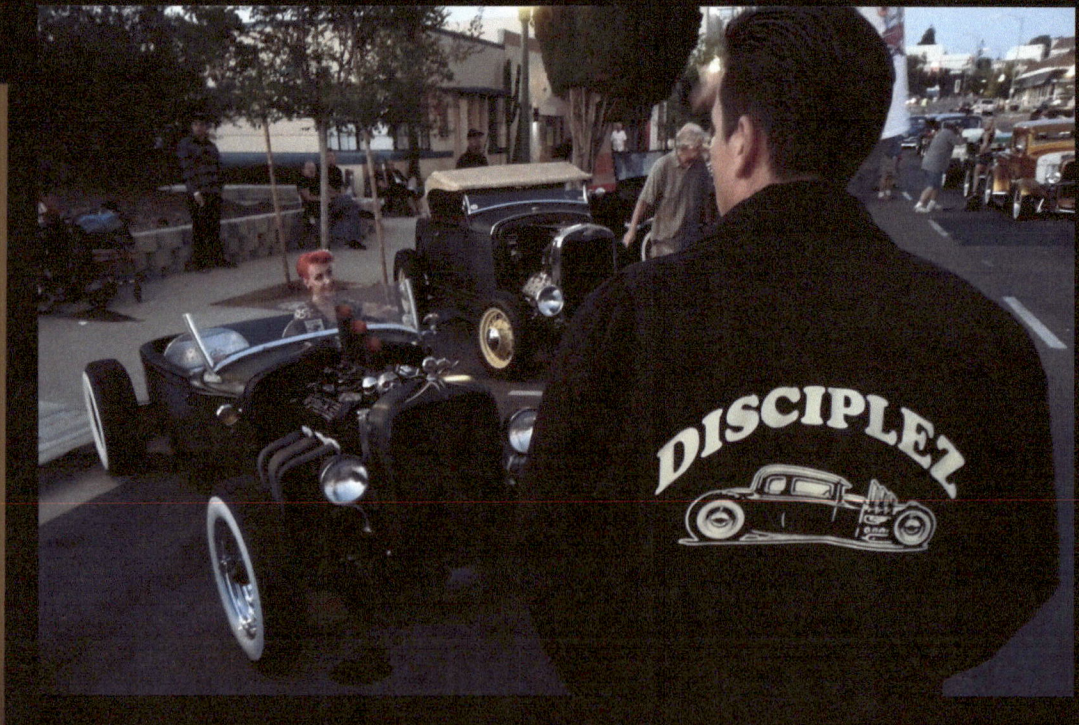

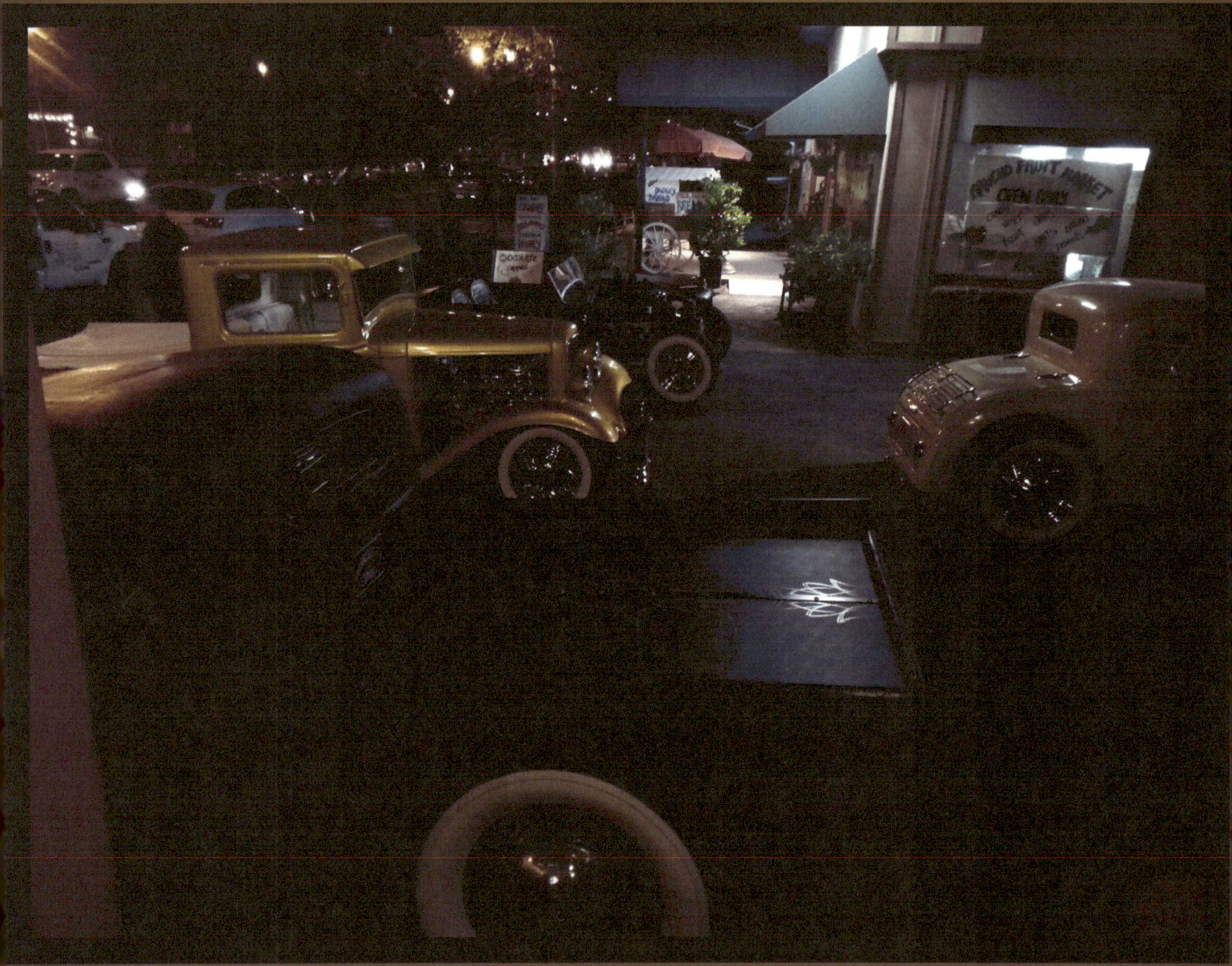

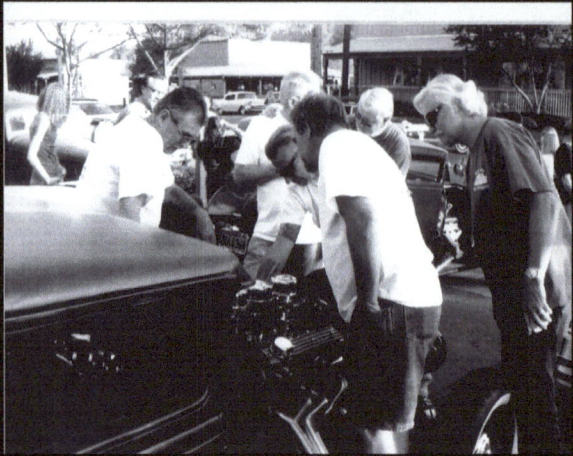

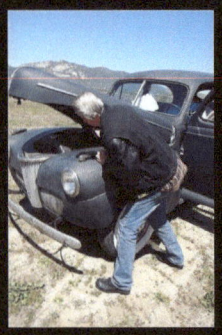

Tribute List

STEVE....................

"LIL C"....................

CHET ....

"ROADSTER BOB".....

"WOODY".................

"PERRIS DAN".........

"CRASH" ....

"DELUXE" ....

ART "KRYPRO".........

"CANDYMAN"..........

CHICK.........

"PREACHER"...........

DAVE & LINDA.......

VICKI.................

"GRITTS".................

"SPIDER".................

JOHNNY........

"HAZ MAT"...............

"BARE METAL DAVE"..

RAY.............

"HARM".................

MARYANNE............

KOSTA....................

"TATTOO GREG"....

"MOTORCYCLE MATT"..

"FLIP".................

HANSI.......................

"WHITE BOY".............

"PONCH"........

"SKREECH".................

"COLONEL DAVE".....

"ONE THUMB".......

www.ingramcontent.com/pod-product-compliance
Lightning Source LLC
Chambersburg PA
CBHW041546040426
42447CB00002B/65